BARBECUE
Chez Bibianne

Happy Barbecuing
Bibianne Robitaille
april 27th 1991

baking and cooking for your outdoor lifestyle

Bibianne Robitaille

Front Cover Photograph
Beef Kebabs, page 29
Shrimp Kebabs, page 29
Herbed Potatoes in Foil, page 55
White and Whole-Wheat Breads, pages 66, 67
Baked Beans, page 58

Barbecue Chez Bibianne
by
Bibianne Robitaille

First Printing - March 1991

Copyright© 1991 by
Chez Bibianne Enterprises Inc.
P.O. Box 50041
14061 Victoria Trail
Edmonton, Alberta
Canada T5Y 2M9

Canadian Cataloguing in Publication Data

Robitaille, Bibianne, 1939-

   Barbecue Chez Bibianne

   ISBN 0-919845-94-0

1. Barbecue cookery.   2. Outdoor cookery.
I. Title.

TX840.B3R62 1991   641.5'784   C91-097074-2

Photography by:
Merle Prosofsky
Merle Prosofsky Photography
Edmonton, Alberta

Barbecue grills and accessories courtesy of:
Barbecues Galore
Edmonton, Alberta

Designed, Printed and Produced in Canada by:
Centax Books, a Division of M•C•Graphics Inc.
Publishing Director, Photo Designer & Food Stylist: Margo Embury
1048 Fleury Street, Regina, Saskatchewan, Canada S4N 4W8
(306)359-3737   FAX (306) 525-3955

Table of Contents

Recipes have been tested in U.S. Standard measurements. Common metric measurements are given as a convenience for those who are more familiar with metric. Recipes have not been tested in metric

Acknowledgments

It would have been impossible for me to write this book without the assistance, encouragement and enthusiasm of my loving husband, Willard, and my three adult children, Bernard, Gérard, and Thérèse. Special thanks to Elnora Kelly whose inspiration and encouragement so contributed to the publishing of this cookbook; to Jeff and Daryl Larsen for their invaluable time and effort on their computer/word processor in the original preparation of the draft copy of this book.

Bibianne Robitaille

Foreword

Why deprive yourself and your guests of all your favorite meals because it's too hot to turn on the oven. With Barbecue Chez Bibianne, you can bake and cook while enjoying your patio, deck, garden, balcony and campsite to the fullest. Enjoy the sunshine, your family and your guests while you prepare complete meals on your barbecue. This book will show you how.

Many of these recipes will become family favorites. We use our barbecue all year round but, if you prefer to use your stove top and oven in the winter, any of these recipes can be prepared on your stove top, in your oven and/or with your broiler.

Barbecue Tips

A. (i) Safety Tips -
Gas/Propane Barbecues

1) Carefully follow your barbecue guide for safety.

2) Never work with flammables around the barbecue.

3) Always wear barbecue mitts to prevent burns.

4) Always use your barbecue in well-ventilated areas.

5) You may use any cookware on your barbecue that you normally use on the top of the stove or in the oven.

6) Never touch any hot cookware on the barbecue without mitts. Remember, even the handles and knobs will be very hot.

7) Never leave the barbecue unattended while baking or cooking.

8) Never leave a young child unsupervised around a hot barbecue.

9) Keep your barbecue grill clean between usages.

10) When performing any flaming (e.g. Cornish Hens Flambé or Chateaubriand), please ensure that this is done at least 6' (2 m) away from a hot barbecue. The dish and food to be flamed, however, must be very hot.

(ii) Safety Tips (Charcoal Barbecues)

1) In addition to the above safety tips, your charcoal barbecue entails specific safety precautions:

   a) Use only approved lighting fluids, especially sold for use on barbecues.

   b) Do not leave charcoal barbecue unattended for a lengthy period of time.

   c) Never throw your charcoal in an ordinary garbage container or cardboard box. Use only a metal container to dispose of your used briquettes.

B. (i) Practical Tips For Barbecue Baking & Cooking - Gas/Propane Barbecues

1) Prepare all your ingredients in advance.

2) Read complete recipe before proceeding with the mixture for cooking or baking. This eliminates any surprises and ensures that each step is faithfully followed.

3) If your barbecue cover does not have a built-in thermometer, an oven thermometer should be purchased at a hardware store (about $5.00).

4) It only takes a few minutes to heat your covered barbecue. Do not light up too early.

5) A heated barbecue does not maintain a constant temperature automatically; therefore, it is important to carefully monitor the temperature and regulate accordingly. Every brand of barbecue is different, so you must adjust yours to regulate the heat.

6) To regulate the temperature, you may have to do one or more of the following:

   a) lower or raise one or both gas valves, if propane or natural gas barbecue is used;

   b) partially open cover, using a metal or stone prop to keep it open;

   c) turn off one gas valve, if required.

7) If water is to be boiled on barbecue, begin with hot tap water and allow extra time for boiling. This is especially important when cooking hard vegetables (e.g. carrots).

8) If you find that specific foods have a tendency to burn on the bottom, elevate the cooking dish to avoid direct heat. This may be accomplished by placing a small stainless steel rack underneath the cooking container. These are normally available at any store which sells barbecue cooking items (about $4.00).

9) Check frequently when baking/cooking to ensure best results and avoid overcooking.

10) You may wish to place a small table adjacent to your barbecue, especially if your barbecue has no adjoining wooden shelves.

(ii) Practical Tips for Barbecue Baking & Cooking - Charcoal Barbecues

In addition to the previous hints for gas/propane barbecues, the following hints relate specifically to charcoal barbecues:

a) You must be more diligent in regulating the heat of a covered barbecue by adding or removing briquettes as required.

b) You will have to be more alert to hot spots on your grill and adjust location of pots accordingly.

C. Advantages of Baking/Cooking on any Barbecue

1) Avoids over-heating your kitchen on a warm day.

2) Certain foods, particularly baking, have a distinctive flavor when done on a barbecue (e.g. homemade bread).

3) It avoids unnecessary and frequent cleaning of your stove, especially your oven.

4) Makes more space available in your kitchen, particularly on stove top and oven.

5) It saves on dirty pots and pans.

6) Allows more opportunities for baking/cooking in fresh air. You can enjoy the sunshine and sit on the deck while cooking and baking.

7) The aroma from your baking/cooking will be the envy of your neighbours (e.g. baking bread, pies or casseroles).

8) It is easier to clean the grill of your barbecue than your stove or oven.

Note: All recipes giving specific "oven" temperatures require cooking with the lid of the barbecue closed.

Notes

Eggs & Cheese

Breakfast in a Pan

1 lb.	bacon	500 g
1 cup	chopped onions	250 mL
3 cups	grated cheddar cheese	750 mL
1⅓ cups	milk	350 mL
3	eggs	3
¾ cup	Tea Biscuit Mix, page 65	175 mL
½ tsp.	salt	2 mL
¼ tsp.	pepper	1 mL

Precook bacon lightly on the barbecue grill and let drain on paper towel. Cut each slice in 4 pieces.

Grease a 9x9" (23x23 cm) pan. Arrange bacon, onions, and ⅔ of the cheese over the bottom of the pan and mix together.

Beat milk, eggs, tea biscuit mix, salt and pepper for 30 seconds. Pour over cheese base, then sprinkle with remaining cheese. **Do not stir.**

Bake on the barbecue at 350°F (180°C), uncovered, for 45 minutes or until a knife pulled out of the center is damp, not wet. Make sure the barbecue cover is closed.

Cooking time: approximately 45 minutes
Serves 5

Bibianne says: Always wear oven or barbecue mitts to save yourself from unnecessary burns.

Poached Eggs in Cheese Sauce

2 cups	Cheese Sauce, page 63	500 mL
6	eggs	6
	paprika	
	parsley	
6 slices	toast	6 slices

Grease a 9x9" (23x23 cm) pan. Pour cheese sauce into pan. Crack eggs into pan, being careful not to break yolks. Sprinkle with paprika and parsley.

Bake on barbecue at 325°F (170°C) for 25 minutes, or until eggs are cooked to your satisfaction. Serve each egg on a slice of toast; spoon sauce over eggs.

Cooking time: approximately 25 minutes
Serves 3

Quiche Bibiana

12	slices of bacon	12
1 cup	shredded mozzarella cheese	250 mL
5	mushrooms, sliced	5
⅓ cup	chopped onions	100 mL
½ cup	Tea Biscuit Mix, page 65	125 mL
4	eggs	4
2 cups	milk	500 mL
¼ tsp.	salt	1 mL
⅛ tsp.	nutmeg	0.5 mL
¼ tsp.	pepper	1 mL

Cook bacon on barbecue grill. Cut or crumble in small pieces. Mix bacon, cheese, mushrooms and chopped onions together in a well-greased deep 9" (23 cm) pie plate.

Place tea biscuit mix, eggs, milk, salt, nutmeg and pepper in blender or bowl and beat for 1 minute on high speed. Pour over base ingredients. **Do not stir.**

Quiche Bibiana
continued

Cook, uncovered, at 450°F (230°C) for 15 minutes. Lower temperature to 300°F (150°C) and cook, uncovered, for another 30 minutes, or until a knife, when inserted into the center, comes out damp, not wet.

Keeps very well, refrigerated, for up to 4 days.

Cooking time: approximately 45 minutes
Serves 5

Macaroni and Cheese

1 cup	macaroni	250 mL
1 tbsp.	vegetable oil	15 mL
¼ cup	chopped onions	60 mL
¼ cup	chopped celery	60 mL
¼ cup	chopped green peppers	60 mL
10 oz.	cream of tomato soup	284 mL
¼ tsp.	white sugar	1 mL
⅛ tsp.	pepper	0.5 mL
⅛ tsp.	salt	0.5 mL
1 cup	grated Cheddar cheese	250 mL

On one end of the barbecue, cook the macaroni according to the instructions on package.

At the other end of barbecue, heat oil in a skillet. Sauté onions, celery and green peppers. Add tomato soup, sugar, pepper and salt; heat through. Add ¾ cup (175 mL) of the cheese; stir until cheese is melted. Add cooked macaroni; stir thoroughly. Sprinkle remaining cheese over macaroni. Bake at 350°F (180°C) for 20 minutes.

Cooking time: approximately 20 minutes
Serves 3

Cheese Soufflé

½ cup	margarine or butter	125 mL
⅓ cup	all-purpose flour	100 mL
1½ cups	milk	375 mL
1½ cups	grated Cheddar cheese	375 mL
⅛ tsp.	pepper	0.5 mL
⅛ tsp.	cayenne	0.5 mL
6	eggs, separated	6

Place a pan containing approximately 1½" (3.5 cm) of water on the barbecue, with the temperature set at 200°F (100°C). The pan must be big enough to hold a 2-quart (2 L) casserole.

In the top portion of a double boiler, melt margarine or butter. Add flour and mix until smooth; add milk gradually, then cheese, pepper and cayenne, stirring until it starts to thicken.

Beat egg yolks until light in color; add slowly to cheese mixture, stirring until it has the consistency of a thick custard.

Beat egg whites until they hold a peak. Fold in cheese mixture with a spatula, being careful not to over mix. Put soufflé batter in a greased 2-quart (2 L) casserole and place casserole in the pan containing the hot water. Bake at 350°F (180°C) for 45 minutes.

Cooking time: approximately 45 minutes
Serves 4

Bibianne says: Do not leave your barbecue unattended for any length of time, especially when you have children around.

Fish & Seafood
Barbecued Stuffed Trout

2	lake trout	2
1 tbsp.	margarine or butter	15 mL
1	carrot, chopped	1
2 tbsp.	chopped green pepper	30 mL
2 tbsp.	chopped celery	30 mL
½ tsp.	dillweed	2 mL
¼ tsp.	salt	1 mL
⅛ tsp.	pepper	0.5 mL
½ cup	cooked rice	125 mL
2 tbsp.	lemon juice	30 mL
2	garlic cloves, sliced	2

Wash trout, pat dry and place on a well-buttered sheet of heavy foil. In a skillet on the barbecue, melt margarine and sauté carrots, green peppers and celery. Add dillweed, salt and pepper. Cook for 1 minute. Stir in rice. Put rice and vegetables in trout cavity. Brush trout with lemon juice. Sprinkle garlic on top.

Wrap fish in foil, leaving seam on top. Bake on barbecue at 300°F (150°C) for 10 minutes. Lower heat to 250°F (120°C) and bake for 45 minutes.

Cooking time: approximately 55 minutes
Serves 2

Grilled Fish Steaks

1 tbsp.	each butter, oil	15 mL
2	1" (2.5 cm) thick fish steaks (any firm-fleshed fish, salmon, swordfish, halibut, etc.)	2

Combine melted butter and oil, brush over fish steaks, both sides. Sprink salt and pepper over steaks and let stand 15-20 minutes. Barbecue on an oiled grill at 375°F (190°), medium-hot, for 3-4 minutes on each side, until fish just flakes with a fork. Serve with a sprinkle of dillweed and fresh lemon.

Cooking time: 3-4 minutes
Serves 2

Sole au Vin

¼ cup	chopped onion	60 mL
¼ cup	chopped celery	60 mL
¼ cup	chopped green pepper	60 mL
1 tbsp.	butter or margarine	15 mL
4	sole filets	4
¼ cup	sour cream	60 mL
½ cup	dry white or nonalcoholic wine	125 mL
	salt and pepper to taste	
½ tsp.	Lemon & Herb Spice	2 mL

Sauté onions, celery and green peppers in margarine or butter in a skillet on the barbecue over medium heat, 350°F (180°C), until tender. Remove sautéed vegetables and set aside.

Using the same skillet, fry the sole filets in butter or margarine until light brown. Spoon vegetables over fish, then pour cream over vegetables and pour wine over all. Add salt, pepper and Lemon & Herb Spice. Cover and simmer gently over a lower temperature, 250°F (120°C), for 15-20 minutes. Serve hot with your favorite rice or potato dish. See photograph on page 17.

Cooking time: approximately 30 minutes
Serves 2

Salmon Steak on Spinach

1 bunch	fresh spinach or 10 oz. (284 g) frozen or 14 oz. (398 g) can	1 bunch
1	hard-boiled egg, sliced	1
3	salmon steaks	3
½ tsp.	curry powder	2 mL
½ tsp.	tarragon	2 mL
	salt and pepper to taste	
4	onion slices	4

Wash fresh spinach thoroughly or drain frozen or canned spinach. In a greased casserole, make a bed of spinach and arrange sliced egg on it. Place salmon steaks side by side over egg slices. Sprinkle with spices. Arrange onions between the salmon steaks. Bake on barbecue at 350°F (180°C) for ½ hour. If it starts boiling, turn down heat. Cook at a simmer.

Cooking time: approximately 30 minutes
Serves 2

Salmon Patties

8	soda crackers	8
7.5 oz.	canned salmon	225 g
¾ cup	mashed potatoes	175 mL
¼ tsp.	each rosemary, thyme	1 mL
⅛ tsp.	pepper	0.5 mL
2 tbsp.	milk	30 mL
1 tsp.	each oil, butter	5 mL
2 tbsp.	chopped onions	30 mL

Put crackers into a plastic bag and, using a rolling pin or jar, crush them. Transfer crumbs to a plate. Drain salmon and reserve liquid for the salmon sauce; add the next 5 ingredients. Mix well and shape into patties. Makes 4-6 patties. Roll each patty in crumbs.

Heat oil and butter in a skillet on the barbecue at 375°F (190°C). Add patties, close barbecue* and brown on both sides. Place onions around patties, not on top. Close barbecue lid. Reduce heat to 250°F (125°C); cook for 15 minutes. Serve with Salmon Sauce, page 62.

* Browning occurs faster on the barbecue with the lid closed. Check after 2-3 minutes and flip patties.

Cooking time: approximately 15 minutes
Serves 2

Salmon Loaf

14 oz.	canned salmon	398 mL
2	slices of bread, cut into fine cubes	2
¼ cup	grated Cheddar cheese	60 mL
1	egg	1
⅛ tsp.	each pepper, salt, rosemary	0.5 mL
	Salmon Sauce, page 62	

Drain salmon and reserve liquid in a measuring cup for the sauce. Flake salmon with a fork; mash in bones for added calcium. Add all other ingredients (not the liquid); mix well. Put in a 8x4" (20x10 cm) loaf pan. Bake at 350°F (180°C) for ½ hour. Serve with Salmon Sauce.

Cooking time: approximately 30 minutes
Serves 3

Seafood Elégant

⅓ lb.	fresh shrimp	150 g
⅓ lb.	fresh scallops	150 g
4	crab sticks	4
2	haddock filets	2
1 tbsp.	butter or margarine	15 mL
1 tbsp.	all-purpose flour	15 mL
⅓ cup	coffee cream (10%)	75 mL
½ cup	sour cream	125 mL
¼ cup	white wine	60 mL
¼ tsp.	paprika	1 mL
2 tbsp.	butter or margarine	30 mL
¼ cup	bread crumbs	60 mL
1 tbsp.	grated Cheddar cheese	15 mL

Chop shrimp and scallops into small pieces. Break the crab sticks and haddock filets into small pieces with your fingers. Place seafood in a buttered casserole.

In a small saucepan, melt 1 tbsp. (15 mL) butter or margarine. Add flour; mix until smooth. Gradually add coffee cream, slowly mixing until it starts to thicken. Add sour cream, wine and paprika gradually. Mix well.

Pour sauce over fish. Melt 2 tbsp. (30 mL) butter or margarine and mix in crumbs. Spread over fish and sprinkle cheese on top. Bake on barbecue at 300°F (150°C) for 40 minutes.

Cooking time: approximately 45 minutes
Serves 3

Bibianne says: Did you know that a 20 lb. (9 kg) propane tank lasts for 24 hours of cooking?

16

Sole au Vin, page 14
Blueberry Pie, page 82
Scalloped Potatoes, page 57

Chicken & Turkey

Barbecued Chicken

6	chicken breasts, boned and skinned	6
¼ cup	vinegar from sweet pickles	60 mL
½ tsp.	dry mustard	2 mL
1	whole garlic clove	1
2 tbsp.	molasses	30 mL
½ tsp.	Worcestershire sauce	2 mL
2 tbsp.	ketchup	30 mL

Wash chicken and pat dry.

Mix remaining ingredients in a small pan and simmer for 2-3 minutes, while stirring frequently.

Brown chicken on barbecue grill. Brush sauce on top part of chicken. Turn chicken, brown and brush sauce on other side of chicken. Do this 3-4 times at 5 minute intervals. Put chicken in a baking pan; pour remaining sauce over meat. Close barbecue lid and cook for ½ hour at 300°F (150°C).

Cooking time: approximately 50 minutes
Serves 3

Bibianne says: Keep a supply of briquettes on hand. You don't want to run out in the middle of your cooking.

19

Roast Chicken Breasts

4	chicken breasts, skin removed	4
¼ cup	water	60 mL
½ tsp.	salt	2 mL
¼ tsp.	pepper	1 mL
½ tsp.	savory	2 mL
1	garlic clove, minced	1
⅓ cup	chopped celery	75 mL
⅓ cup	chopped onion	75 mL
1 cup	sliced fresh mushrooms	250 mL
1 cup	sliced carrots	250 mL
1 cup	green beans	250 mL

Wash chicken breasts, place side by side in baking pan. Add water. Sprinkle spices over the chicken. Cook chicken ½ hour, covered, at 275°F (140°C) with barbecue lid closed.

Sprinkle celery and onions over the chicken, cover and cook for another hour. Add fresh mushrooms, carrots and green beans. Cover and cook for ½ hour, or until vegetables are cooked.

Cooking time: approximately 2 hours
Serves 4

Hot Garlic Chicken Wings

2 lbs.	chicken wings	1 kg
2-3	garlic cloves, minced	2-3
1	lemon, juice of	1
2-3	green onions, thinly sliced	2-3
¼ cup	vegetable oil	60 mL
½ tsp.	dry mustard	2 mL
½ tsp.	paprika	2 mL
¼-1 tsp.	cayenne pepper	1-5 mL
¼-1 tsp.	crushed chili peppers	1-5 mL
½ tsp.	Tabasco sauce	2 mL
½ tsp.	Worcestershire sauce	2 mL
2 tsp.	brown sugar	10 mL
	salt and pepper to taste	

Hot Garlic Chicken Wings
continued

Remove wing tips and cut wings in half at the joint, if you wish, or fold them back to make triangle shapes. Combine remaining ingredients and marinate wings for 2 hours to overnight.

Cook wings on the grill at 375°F (190°C) for 5-8 minutes per side, basting when turning.

Variation: Try this marinade with chicken thighs or drumsticks — increase cooking time to 15-20 minutes per side.

Variation: Try adding ¼ cup (60 mL) of soy sauce and ½ tsp. (2 mL) of ground ginger to the marinade.

Cooking time: 10-16 minutes
Serves 4

Honey Peach Chicken

8	chicken thighs, skin removed	8
½ tsp.	cayenne	2 mL
3 tbsp.	peach jam	45 mL
2 tsp.	Worcestershire sauce	10 mL
½ tsp.	salt	2 mL
¼ cup	vinegar from sweet pickles	60 mL
½ tsp.	dry mustard	2 mL
2	garlic cloves, finely chopped	2
2 tbsp.	liquid honey	30 mL

Wash chicken and set aside to drain.

In an ovenproof glass casserole, combine remaining ingredients. Place chicken in sauce; cover and let it marinate for at least 8 hours or up to 36 hours, turning it at least 2 or 3 times.

Bake chicken in the marinade, in the same casserole, covered, on the barbecue with the lid closed, at 350°F (180°C) until it boils, about 20 minutes. Lower heat to 275°F (130°C) and gently simmer for 2 hours. Remove casserole cover for the last 25 minutes and let brown. Keep barbecue lid closed for entire cooking time.

Cooking time: approximately 2½ hours
Serves 4

Fried Chicken

3 lbs.	drumsticks	1.5 kg
2½ cups	cornflakes	625 mL
1 tsp.	salt	5 mL
½ tsp.	pepper	2 mL
½ tsp.	savory	2 mL
½ tsp.	dillweed	2 mL
¼ tsp.	poultry seasoning	1 mL
½ cup	all-purpose flour	125 mL
1	egg	1
2 tbsp.	milk	30 mL
3 tbsp.	butter or margarine	45 mL
2 tbsp.	vegetable oil	30 mL

Wash chicken and pat dry.

Crush cornflakes very fine, add salt, pepper, savory, dillweed and poultry seasoning. Put in plastic bag and set aside. Put flour in a different plastic bag and set aside.

Beat egg and milk together in a bowl.

Shake chicken first in flour, then roll in egg mixture and lastly shake in cornflakes.

In a skillet on the barbecue at 350°F (180°C), heat butter or margarine and oil. Brown chicken on all sides, about 5 minutes per side. Keep barbecue cover closed when not turning chicken. After drumsticks are browned, place them in a shallow pan or on a cookie sheet and cook, with lid closed, for another 45 minutes, with temperature set at 275°F (140°C). See page 6 to regulate heat.

Cooking time: approximately 1 hour
Serves 4

Chicken Cordon Bleu

½ tsp.	salt	2 mL
½ tsp.	poultry seasoning	2 mL
½ tsp.	savory	2 mL
¼ tsp.	pepper	1 mL
½ cup	bread crumbs	125 mL
½ cup	all-purpose flour	125 mL
1	egg	1
2 tbsp.	milk	30 mL
6	half chicken breasts, boned & skinned	6
3	thin ham slices, cut in half	3
3	thin Swiss cheese slices, cut in half	3
½ cup	water	125 mL
2 tbsp.	butter or margarine	30 mL
1 tbsp.	vegetable oil	15 mL

Combine first 5 ingredients in a shallow dish and set aside.

Put flour in a different shallow dish and set aside.

Beat egg and milk together in a bowl with a fork.

Wash chicken and pat dry. Lay chicken on a flat surface and sprinkle with salt and pepper. Put a ½ slice of ham and cheese on each breast, roll and secure with toothpicks or skewers.

Roll chicken firstly in flour, then in egg mixture, and lastly in bread crumbs. Heat butter or margarine and oil in a skillet on the barbecue with temperature set at 350°F (180°C). Brown chicken on all sides, add water, sprinkle with salt and pepper. Lower temperature to 250°F (120°C), close barbecue lid and simmer gently for ½ hour.

Cooking time: approximately 45 minutes
Serves 6

Roast Chicken

5 lb.	roasting chicken	2.5 kg
2-3 cups	stuffing, pages 70, 73	500-750 mL
1 cup	water	250 mL

Wash chicken in cold water and let drain. Prepare your favorite stuffing recipe or use a recipe on pages 70, 73. Place stuffing inside cavity. Put chicken in a roasting pan, add water, cover.

Cook on barbecue at low heat, 300°F (150°C) with barbecue lid closed. Cook ½ hour per pound (500 g). If chicken does not brown, remove roasting pan lid for the last 20 minutes of cooking, but keep lid of barbecue closed or partially closed to control heat.

Cooking time: approximately ½ hour per pound (500 g)
Serves 5

Cornish Hens Flambé

4	Cornish hens	4
¼ cup	wild rice	60 mL
¼ cup	white rice	60 mL
2 tbsp.	amaretto	30 mL

Remove neck, liver, etc. from inside hens. Wash hens and let drain.

Cook both rices together according to instructions on wild rice package. Stuff each hen with cooked rice and put in a shallow pan, side by side. Cover bottom of pan with water.

Cover pan and cook at 300°F (150°C) with barbecue lid closed for 45 minutes. With a pastry brush, brush hens with amaretto. Lower heat to 250°F (120°C) and cook, uncovered, for 1 hour. Do this to cook them slowly. They have to simmer gently. If the pan gets dry, add a bit of water.

Just before serving, for safety, place cooked hens a safe distance from barbecue. Make sure they are hot. Pour the leftover amaretto on hens and light with a long match.

Note: Keep amaretto in a closed container to prevent evaporation.

Cooking time: approximately 1 hour 45 minutes
Serves 4

Chicken & Dumplings Stew

3 lb.	stewing chicken	1.5 kg
1	large onion	1
2	bay leaves	2
1 tsp.	salt	5 mL
½ tsp.	pepper	2 mL
¼ tsp.	savory	1 mL
4	carrots, cut in pieces	4
½	turnip, cut in small pieces	½

Wash chicken and remove skin. Put in a 4-quart (4 L) saucepan and cover with water. Cut onion into quarters and add to chicken along with all of the spices; cover.

Put chicken on barbecue with temperature set at 375°F (190°C). Close barbecue lid. Bring chicken to a boil. If using cold water, allow ½ hour longer. When chicken boils, reduce heat to 225°F (110°C) and let simmer for 2 hours, or until chicken is almost cooked. If it continues to boil, lower temperature.* Add vegetables and simmer for 20 minutes.

Please note: If water isn't level with top of chicken, dumplings won't cook as well. Water has to simmer before you put in the dumplings. Do **not** put water above the top of the chicken.

Prepare dumplings, page 69. Drop batter by spoonfuls on vegetables and chicken; cover pot and close barbecue lid; simmer for 15 minutes. No peeking please.

* The recipe can be made up to this point the day before. Add the vegetables in time to finish cooking for your meal.

See photograph on page 53.

Cooking time: approximately 3 hours
Serves 4

Chicken Pot Pie

1 lb.	cooked chicken, cubed	500 g
2 tbsp.	chopped onions	30 mL
¼ tsp.	salt	1 mL
⅛ tsp.	pepper	0.5 mL
⅛ tsp.	poultry seasoning	0.5 mL
½ cup	warm gravy	125 mL
1 cup	Pie Crust Mix, page 81	250 mL
1 tbsp.	milk	15 mL

Combine first 6 ingredients. If you desire more moisture, add more gravy.

Combine pie crust mix with water or sour milk. Roll crust to fit a 2-quart (2 L) size casserole, plus enough to have 2" (5 cm) overlap all around. Place chicken mixture inside crust. Fold extra crust over chicken, leaving an opening in the middle for steam to escape. Brush crust with milk.

Bake at 400°F (200°C), with barbecue lid closed, for 10-15 minutes or until crust starts to brown. Lower temperature to 300°F (150°C) for 20 minutes.

Cooking time: approximately 35 minutes
Serves 3

Roast Turkey

10 lb.	turkey	4.5 kg
	salt & pepper	
5-7 cups	stuffing	1.25-1.75 L
½ cup	water	125 mL

Wash turkey and let drain. Sprinkle the inside of the turkey with salt and pepper. Stuff with your favorite stuffing or use a recipe, pages 70-73. Place turkey in a roasting pan, add water and cover. Roast on barbecue, with lid closed, set at 300°F (150°C), for 25 minutes per pound or 55 minutes per kg.

The cooking time will be less if stuffing isn't used. (About 20 minutes per pound or 45 minutes per kg.)

Cooking time: approximately 4 hours 15 minutes
Serves 15

Turkey à la King

1 cup	thick gravy	250 mL
⅓ cup	cereal cream (10%)	100 mL
½ tsp.	salt	2 mL
¼ tsp.	pepper	1 mL
¼ tsp.	dry mustard	1 mL
1½ lbs.	cooked turkey	750 kg
6	puffed pastry shells	6

In a pan on the barbecue, combine gravy, cream, salt, pepper and mustard; simmer for 2 minutes.

Cut the turkey into small pieces and mix into the sauce. Simmer for 2-3 minutes until turkey is very hot. Serve hot in warm puffed pastry shells.

Cooking time: approximately 5 minutes
Serves 3-5

Turkey Croquettes

1½ lbs.	cooked turkey	750 g
2	eggs	2
1 cup	mashed potatoes	250 mL
2 tbsp.	milk	30 mL
1 tsp.	salt	5 mL
½ tsp.	pepper	2 mL
½ tsp.	poultry seasoning	2 mL
½ cup	finely chopped onions	125 mL
¾ cup	bread crumbs	175 mL
3 tbsp.	butter or margarine	45 mL

Grind turkey; add the next 7 ingredients and mix well. With your hands, roll turkey mixture into tube shapes about 3" (7.5 cm) long and 2" (5 cm) in circumference. Roll croquettes in bread crumbs.

Melt butter or margarine in a frying pan on the barbecue, with temperature set at 400°F (200°C) and brown croquettes on all sides. This takes about 15 minutes. Lower heat to 275°F (140°C). Close barbecue lid and cook for ½ hour. If you find pan somewhat dry, add just enough water to cover bottom of pan.

Cooking time: approximately 45 minutes
Makes 8-10 croquettes

Notes

Beef

Beef Kebabs

¾ lb.	sirloin steak	350 g
2 tbsp.	dry red or nonalcoholic wine	30 mL
1	bay leaf	1
1	garlic clove, minced	1
⅛ tsp.	crushed tarragon leaves	0.5 mL
½ tsp.	Worcestershire sauce	2 mL
12	cherry tomatoes	12
12	mushrooms, stems removed	12
12	square pieces of green pepper	12
12	square pieces of onion	12
1 tsp.	lemon juice	5 mL
1 tsp.	cornstarch	5 mL
	cooked rice	

Cut steak in 1½" (4 cm) square pieces, about 12 pieces. In a glass bowl, mix next 5 ingredients. Add meat and let marinate for 4-5 hours, turning 4-5 times.

Use 4 skewers. On each, alternate vegetables and steak and continue until all meat and vegetables are used. Set barbecue to 400°F (200°C), place skewers on skewer stand. Place skewer stand on barbecue. Cook for 6 minutes for rare, 9 minutes for medium and 10 minutes for well done, turning skewers halfway through cooking time.

In a small saucepan combine marinade sauce, lemon juice and cornstarch; stir over heat until simmering and slightly thickened. Pour sauce over a bed of rice and carefully slide kebabs onto rice.

Variation: For quick Seafood Kebabs, marinate shrimp, scallops, halibut, cod or snapper for about 30 minutes in Oriental Marinade, page 59, or an oil and lemon dressing with 1 tsp. (5 mL) crushed oregano and 1 minced garlic clove. Proceed as for Beef Kebabs; cook about 6-10 minutes.

See photograph on front cover.

Cooking time: approximately 6-10 minutes
Serves 2

Steak & Vegetables

1½ lbs.	blade steak	750 g
½ tsp.	salt	2 mL
⅛ tsp.	pepper	0.5 mL
1 tsp.	Worcestershire sauce	5 mL
3	garlic cloves	3
2	medium onions	2
3	medium carrots	3
9	green string beans	9
2	celery sticks	2
3	small potatoes	3

Brown steak on grill. Then place it in a 2" (5 cm) high skillet. Sprinkle steak with salt, pepper and Worcestershire sauce. Cut garlic cloves into 3-4 pieces and put them on meat. Cut onions into quarters and put around meat. Add approximately ¼" (6 mm) of water in the bottom of the skillet. Cover and simmer for 1 hour at 250°F (120°C).

Slice vegetables and add to meat. Keep water level to ¼" (6 mm). Simmer for ½ hour or until vegetables are cooked.

Cooking time: approximately 1½ hours
Serves 3

Bibianne says: Use the barbecue and keep your stove clean.

Chateaubriand

| 3 lbs. | beef tenderloin | 1.5 kg |
| 2 tbsp. | very warm brandy | 30 mL |

Place meat on barbecue grill, with barbecue set at 500°F (260°C). Well done: 60 minutes; Medium: 45 minutes; Rare: 30 minutes. Turn meat periodically so it will brown on all sides.

When meat is cooked, remove it a safe distance from the barbecue. Leave it in the hot pan, pour the warm brandy over hot meat and light with a long match. Serve with Béarnaise Sauce, recipe below.

Béarnaise Sauce

3	egg yolks	3
5 tbsp.	lemon juice	75 mL
⅔ cup	cold butter or margarine	150 mL
3 tbsp.	dry white wine	45 mL
1	green onion, chopped	1
1 tsp.	sweet basil	5 mL
¼ tsp.	oregano	1 mL

While meat is cooking, prepare the sauce. In the top of a double boiler, beat the egg yolks and lemon juice very fast with a whisk or wooden spoon. Add ½ of the cold butter or margarine. Over low heat, stir until margarine is melted. Keep the water in the double boiler below the boiling point. If water starts to boil, add 1 or 2 tsp. (5 or 10 mL) of cold water. Add remaining butter or margarine and stir until sauce thickens. Sauce has to cook slowly, below the boiling point, to prevent eggs from curdling. Slowly stir in the wine, onions, basil and oregano. Continue cooking until very hot, about 5 minutes. Cover and keep warm until serving time. Serve with meat.

Cooking time: approximately 30-60 minutes
Serves 5

Bibianne says: Do not work with flammables around your barbecue.

Stuffed Rouladen

4	rouladen*	4
¼ tsp.	salt	1 mL
⅛ tsp.	pepper	0.5 mL
¼ tsp.	oregano	1 mL
⅓ recipe	Bread Stuffing #1, page 70	⅓ recipe
¼ cup	water	60 mL

Unroll rouladen, sprinkle each with salt, pepper and oregano. Place stuffing on each rouladen, roll and secure with a toothpick. Place rouladen side by side in a casserole, add the water and cover. Bake at 300°F (180°C) for 40 minutes.

* 3x4" (7x10 cm) thin rectangles of pounded flank, round or sirloin steak.

Cooking time: approximately 40 minutes
Serves 2

Bibianne says: Take your time — relax when you are cooking on the barbecue. Time improves the flavor of your dishes.

Veal Cordon Bleu

½ tsp.	allspice	2 mL
1	garlic clove, minced	1
½ tsp.	salt	2 mL
¼ tsp.	pepper	1 mL
½ cup	bread crumbs	125 mL
½ cup	all-purpose flour	125 mL
1	egg	1
2 tbsp.	milk	30 mL
6	veal cutlets	6
3	slices cooked ham, cut in half	3
3	slices Swiss cheese, cut in half	3
3 tbsp.	butter or margarine	45 mL
¾ cup	water	175 mL

Mix first 5 ingredients in shallow dish and set aside.

Put flour in shallow dish and set aside.

Beat egg and milk in a bowl with a fork.

Spread cutlets on a flat surface and sprinkle with salt and pepper. Put a ½ slice of ham and cheese on each. Roll and secure with toothpicks or skewers. Roll each in flour, then in egg mixture and, finally, bread crumb mixture.

Melt butter or margarine in a frying pan on the barbecue. Add the cutlets, close the barbecue cover and brown on all sides at 400°F (200°C). Browning takes about 10 minutes, close cover again after turning rolls. Add the water, close lid and cook on low heat at 300°F (150°C) for 30 minutes.

Cooking time: approximately 30 minutes
Serves 6

Sweet & Sour Meatballs

1 lb.	ground beef	500 g
¼ cup	bread crumbs	60 mL
2 tbsp.	milk	30 mL
⅛ tsp.	pepper	0.5 mL
⅛ tsp.	salt	0.5 mL
½ cup	vinegar from sweet pickles	125 mL
2 tbsp.	brown sugar	30 mL
3 tbsp.	ketchup	45 mL
⅛ tsp.	prepared mustard	0.5 mL
2	whole garlic cloves, chopped	2
1 tsp.	Worcestershire sauce	5 mL

Mix first 5 ingredients together and shape into small meatballs, approximately 22-25. Put in skillet. Place skillet on the barbecue with temperature set at 350°F (180°C) and brown all sides. Drain off fat.

In a 1½-quart (1.5 L) casserole, combine remaining ingredients and add meatballs. Simmer gently for 1 hour with temperature set at 250°F (120°C). This recipe freezes very well.

Cooking time: approximately 1 hour
Serves 3

Bibianne says: Organize yourself and save work.

Barbecued Spareribs, page 43
Pizza, page 48

Meatballs Bourguignonne

¼ cup	all-purpose flour	60 mL
1¼ lb.	lean ground beef	625 g
⅓ cup	bread crumbs	75 mL
½ tsp.	salt	2 mL
¼ tsp.	pepper	1 mL
1	egg	1
1 cup	dry red or nonalcoholic wine	250 mL
1 cup	water	250 mL
¼ tsp.	salt	1 mL
⅛ tsp.	pepper	0.5 mL
2	garlic cloves, halved	2
2	bay leaves	2
3	medium onions, quartered	3
4	medium potatoes, quartered	4
4	medium carrots, sliced	4
2	celery sticks cut into 1½" (3.5 cm) lengths	2
10	small mushrooms	10

Put flour on a plate. In a mixing bowl, add the next 5 ingredients and mix well. Shape mixture into 15-20 meatballs. Roll them in the flour.

Set temperature on barbecue to 350°F (180°C). Oil the bottom of a 3-4-quart (3-4 L) pan or Dutch oven. Place meatballs in the pan and brown on all sides, about 15 minutes. Drain off any fat before adding other ingredients.

Add next 6 ingredients, simmer for 1 hour and 15 minutes, stirring 2-3 times.* Add remaining ingredients; simmer for ½ hour or until vegetables are cooked. Remove garlic cloves and bay leaves before serving.

* The recipe can be made up to this point and frozen. It can also be made a day ahead. Just add the vegetables in time to finish cooking for your meal.

Cooking time: approximately 2 hours
Serves 5

Stuffed Meat Loaf

3	slices of bread	3
1 tbsp.	chopped onion	15 mL
2 tbsp.	chopped celery	30 mL
¼ tsp.	thyme	1 mL
¼ tsp.	salt	1 mL
⅛ tsp.	pepper	0.5 mL
1 lb.	ground beef	500 g
1	egg	1
½ cup	bread crumbs	125 mL
1 tbsp.	ketchup	15 mL
1 tsp.	mustard	5 mL
2 tbsp.	chopped onion	30 mL

Wet bread and squeeze out water. Break bread into small pieces. Mix with the next 5 ingredients to make dressing and set aside.

Mix ground beef and remaining ingredients together.

On a small cookie sheet or metal pie plate, put ⅔ of the meat mixture and shape it into a loaf. The loaf should be about 4" (10 cm) wide and 7" (17.5 cm) long. Make a well on top of the loaf and put in the stuffing. Cover it with the remaining meat. Bake on the barbecue, with the lid closed, for 1 hour, with temperature set at 325°F (160°C).

Cooking time: approximately 1½ hours
Serves 4

Bibianne says: Always read the whole recipe before you start cooking.

Chile Con Carne

1 lb.	ground beef	500 g
⅓ cup	chopped celery	75 mL
¼ cup	chopped onion	60 mL
1 slice	bacon, cooked & chopped	1 slice
3 tbsp.	water	45 mL
¼ tsp.	oregano	1 mL
¼ tsp.	sweet basil	1 mL
¼ tsp.	dried crushed chilies	1 mL
	salt and pepper to taste	
½ cup	ketchup*	125 mL
14 oz.	can red kidney beans	398 mL

Brown meat in a 1½-quart (1.5 L) saucepan. Add next 8 ingredients; simmer for 15 minutes. Add ketchup and beans; simmer for 20 minutes.

Variation: For a milder version, spice with ⅛ tsp. (0.5 mL) black pepper, ¼ tsp. (1 mL) thyme and ⅛ tsp. (0.5 mL) crushed chilies instead of the oregano, sweet basil and ¼ tsp. (1 mL) crushed chilies listed above. Also, substitute a 10 oz. (284 mL) can of tomato soup for the ketchup.

For a spicy version, increase the amount of crushed chili pepper, up to 1-2 tsp. or more, to your taste.

* Substitute a 14 oz. (398 mL) can of tomatoes and 7½ oz. (213 mL) of tomato sauce for ketchup, if you prefer.

See photograph on back cover.

Cooking time: approximately 53 minutes
Serves 3

Shepherd's Pie

1⅓ lbs.	lean ground beef	600 g
1 tsp.	salt	5 mL
¼ tsp.	crushed oregano leaves	1 mL
¼ tsp.	thyme	1 mL
⅛ tsp.	pepper	0.5 mL
14 oz.	can of cream corn	398 mL
4	thin onion slices	4
2 cups	mashed potatoes	500 mL
2 tbsp.	butter or margarine	30 mL
3 tbsp.	bread crumbs	45 mL
2 tbsp.	grated Cheddar cheese	30 mL

In a skillet, brown meat lightly and drain off fat.

Transfer meat to a 2-quart (2 L) casserole; sprinkle with salt, oregano, thyme and pepper; spread cream corn over meat and spices. Arrange onion rings over corn. Scoop potatoes over onions. With the back of a spoon, spread potatoes evenly.

In the skillet, melt butter or margarine, add bread crumbs and mix well. Sprinkle over potatoes, then sprinkle with grated Cheddar cheese. Bake on barbecue at 325°F (170°C), with lid closed, for ½ hour to 45 minutes, until meat is cooked.

Cooking time: approximately 45 minutes
Serves 4

Macaroni & Hamburger Casserole

1 cup	macaroni	250 mL
½ cup	chopped onion	125 mL
½ cup	chopped celery	125 mL
½ cup	chopped green pepper	125 mL
½ tsp.	butter or margarine	2 mL
1 lb.	lean hamburger	500 g
10 oz.	tomato soup	284 mL
1 tsp.	Italian seasoning	5 mL
1 tsp.	salt	5 mL
1 tsp.	black pepper	5 mL

Macaroni & Hamburger Casserole
continued

Put the water for the macaroni on the barbecue to boil while you prepare the other ingredients.Cook macaroni according to package instructions.

Sauté onions, celery, and green peppers in melted butter or margarine in a skillet. Set aside.

Using the same skillet, brown meat over medium heat. Add sautéed vegetables, soup, Italian dressing, cooked macaroni and spices. Mix well. Cover skillet and cook over low heat, 250°F (120°C), on barbecue for 40 minutes, with lid closed.

Cooking time: approximately 50 minutes
Serves 4

Meat Roll

1 lb.	**leftover roast beef**	**500 g**
1 tsp.	**salt**	**5 mL**
½ tsp.	**thyme**	**2 mL**
3 tbsp.	**chopped onion**	**45 mL**
½ cup	**beef gravy**	**125 mL**
¼ tsp.	**pepper**	**1 mL**
1¼ cups	**Pie Crust Mix, page 80**	**300 mL**
	milk	

Grind beef, add remaining ingredients, except for the pie crust and milk.

Prepare pie crust by adding water or sour milk. Using a rolling pin, roll out crust to 12x8" (31x20 cm.)

Spread meat mixture on the crust, leaving some space on edges. Roll like a jelly roll and seal seam with water. Brush top with milk.

Put roll on a cookie sheet. Place on barbecue, close lid and bake at 400°F (200°C) for 10 minutes. Lower heat to 375°F (190°C) and cook for another 20 minutes.

Keeps very well, refrigerated, up to 3 days.

Cooking time: approximately 30 minutes
Serves 5

Tourtière

3½ lbs.	ground extra lean pork	1.75 kg
2¼ lbs.	ground extra lean beef	1 kg
1-3 tsp.	savory	5-15 mL
1-3 tsp.	thyme	5-15 mL
1½-3 tsp.	salt	7-15 mL
½-1½ tsp.	pepper	2-7 mL
3 tbsp.	water	45 mL
3-5	garlic cloves, minced (optional)	3-5
3	2-crust pie shells, page 80	3
	milk	

Place meat and water in a large pan and cover. Place on barbecue, set at 225°F (110°C). Simmer very gently for 3 hours, stirring occasionally. It is very important that the meat is well cooked and not lumpy. Drain off fat as it accumulates. Add seasonings to taste, for a milder flavour use the first amount, for a spicier version increase the amount of spices.

Line pie plates with pastry and fill each crust with meat. Cover each with top crust. Make a few slits for steam to escape. Brush the top crust with milk. Bake at 400°F (200°C) on the barbecue, with lid down for 15 minutes, or until the top crust is brown. Lower the heat to 350°F (180°C) for 20 minutes.

These pies freeze very well before or after baking.

Tourtiére is a traditional Christmas meat pie that has its origins in French Canada. It is enjoyed by food lovers of all ethnic/national origins. It is not highly spiced, if you use the first amount of spice suggested, and the addition of beef is welcomed by those who can not eat pure pork. It is delicious and is a welcome treat at any time of the year.

Variations: Variations of Tourtiére abound, add 2-3 cups (500-750 mL) of finely chopped onion and 1 tbsp. (15 mL) sage to the above ingredients. Try substituting 1 tbsp. (15 mL) cinnamon, 2 tsp. (10 mL) nutmeg, 2 tsp. (10 mL) allspice and 2 tsp. (10 mL) cloves for the savory, thyme and garlic.

Cooking time: 3 hours, 35 minutes
Serves 18
To make 1 pie adjust amount of ingredients accordingly

Pork

Barbecued Spareribs

3½ lbs.	pork side ribs	1.5 kg
¾ cup	vinegar from sweet pickles	175 mL
½ tsp.	mustard	2 mL
2 tbsp.	brown sugar	30 mL
½ cup	ketchup	125 mL
2	garlic cloves, chopped	2
2 tsp.	Worcestershire sauce	10 mL

Separate each rib and brown on barbecue grill on both sides.

While ribs are browning, on the opposite end of the barbecue in a small saucepan, combine the next 6 ingredients. Simmer for 2-3 minutes.

Dip ribs in sauce and brown again on medium heat. Do this 3 times. You may also brush ribs with sauce as you brown and turn them. Do this 3 times.

Put ribs in shallow pan and pour remaining sauce over them. Lower heat to 250°F (120°C), close barbecue lid; cook for 30 minutes. If sauce evaporates too quickly, cover pan to finish cooking.

See photograph on page 36.

Cooking time: approximately 30-35 minutes
Serves 5

Stuffed Roast of Pork

3 lb.	rolled pork roast	1.5 kg
1½ cups	Bread Stuffing #1, page 70	375 mL
½ cup	water	125 mL

Unroll roast. Spread dressing over meat, reroll and tie with butcher's cord. Put on grill and brown all around, being careful not to burn the cord.

Put roast in roasting pan, add water, cover. Place on barbecue, close lid and cook at 300°F (150°C) for 50 minutes per pound (105 minutes per kg).

Cooking time: approximately 2 hours, 45 minutes
Serves 6

Stuffed Pork Chops

2	pork loin chops 1¼" (3 cm) thick	2
2 tsp.	vegetable oil	10 mL
¼ cup	chopped carrot	60 mL
¼ cup	chopped onion	60 mL
¼ cup	chopped green pepper	60 mL
⅛ tsp.	salt	1 mL
⅛ tsp.	sage	1 mL

Slice a pocket opposite the bone side of each chop. Put chops on the grill to brown.

In a frying pan on the barbecue, add the oil, and sauté the vegetables and spices. Cook until the vegetables are ½ done.

After chops are brown on both sides, spoon the vegetables into the pockets and return them to the same pan. Add water to just cover the bottom of the pan. Lower heat to 225°F (110°C), cover pan, close barbecue lid and cook for 30 minutes.

Cooking time: approximately 45 minutes
Serves 2

Pork Tenderloin

1½ lbs.	pork tenderloin	750 g
½ cup	bread crumbs	125 mL
¼ tsp.	sweet basil	1 mL
¼ tsp.	salt	1 mL
¼ tsp.	pepper	1 mL
¼ tsp.	oregano	1 mL
¼ cup	milk	60 mL
2 tbsp.	butter or margarine	30 mL
¼ cup	water	60 mL

Cut tenderloin into 1½" (4 cm) thick slices.

Mix next 5 ingredients together in a plastic bag.

Dip tenderloin in milk, drain and shake in prepared crumbs, until evenly coated.

Melt butter or margarine in a skillet on the barbecue, with temperature set at 350°F (180°C). Add meat, close barbecue cover. Brown tenderloin slices on both sides, about 5 minutes per side. Add water, cover skillet and simmer at 250°F (120°C) for 30 minutes.

Cooking time: approximately 45 minutes
Serves 4

Bibianne says: Always follow your manufacturer's barbecue guide for safety.

Baked Ham

4 lbs.	ham	2 kg

Put ham into a 3-quart (3 L) pan, ½ filled with water. Simmer for 1½ hours on barbecue set at 350°F (180°C) with lid closed. Transfer ham to a roasting pan, cover pan, place on barbecue, close lid and bake for 30 minutes per lb. (500 g) at 300°F (150°C).

Decorate ham if you desire, or you can brush it with a glaze periodically while baking. Glaze recipe below.

Honey Mustard Glaze

¼ cup	liquid honey	60 mL
2 tsp.	prepared mustard	10 mL
2 tsp.	hot ham liquid	10 mL

Combine all ingredients; brush ham 2-3 times while baking.

Cooking time: approximately 3 hours 30 minutes
With bone, serves 5; without bone, serves 8

Ham Kebabs

2-2½ lb.	baked cubed ham, 1½" (4 cm) cubes orange wedges, with peel pineapple chunks, mushrooms, green pepper	4 kg

Orange Sauce

½ cup	extra-hot ketchup	125 mL
⅓ cup	orange marmalade	75 mL
2 tbsp.	finely chopped onion	30 mL
2 tbsp.	vegetable oil	30 mL
1 tbsp.	lemon juice	15 mL
1-1½ tsp.	dry mustard	5-7 mL

Thread ham, fruit and vegetables alternately on skewers. Combine sauce ingredients. Put kebabs on barbecue over low coals. Brush with sauce; turn often to cook evenly.

Variation: Substitute spiced crabapples for mushrooms and green peppers.

Cooking time: 12-15 minutes
Serves 6

Pasta Plus

Spaghetti & Meat Sauce

1½ lb.	lean ground beef	750 g
2	celery stalks	2
10	medium mushrooms	10
⅓	medium green pepper	⅓
3	large garlic cloves, minced	3
½ tsp.	sugar	2 mL
2 tsp.	Italian seasoning	10 mL
⅛ tsp.	chili powder	0.5 mL
13 oz.	tomato paste	369 mL
48 oz.	tomato juice	1.36 L

Turn barbecue on with temperature set at 350°F (180°C). Brown meat lightly in pan, stirring a few times so meat doesn't stick.

Chop all vegetables, add to meat and then add all remaining ingredients and stir. Cover pan and lower temperature to 300°F (150°C). When sauce starts to simmer, bring heat down to 250°F (120°C). If it starts to boil, turn heat down even more. If it starts to stick to the pan, elevate pan off the grill. See Tips, page 6.

Cook sauce 4 hours, stirring frequently. Can be simmered gently up to 8 hours to improve flavor and thickness. This sauce freezes very well.

Cooking time: approximately 6-8 hours
Serves 8

Pizza

1 cup	scalded milk	250 mL
4 tsp.	fast-rising yeast	20 mL
1 tbsp.	soft margarine	15 mL
1	egg	1
½ tsp.	salt	2 mL
3-4 cups	all-purpose flour	750 mL-1 L

To scald milk, put milk in a saucepan and heat until you see little bubbles along the side. Remove from heat and cool to lukewarm.To the milk add yeast, margarine, egg and salt. Beat with a mixer for 1 minute. Continue beating while slowly adding flour. Use a spoon when the mixer has difficulty mixing. Turn dough onto floured counter or table and knead 4-5 minutes. Check page 67 for kneading instructions. Let rise until it doubles in bulk. Oil 2 large pizza pans. Turn dough onto floured surface; divide in half. With oily finger tips, lift dough and let it hang while turning it. Be careful not to tear it in the middle. Keep your finger tips oiled and put dough in middle of pans. Spread dough while pressing gently and pushing towards the edge of the pan. Keep going around until pan is covered. Use your favorite toppings, see below. Bake on barbecue at 425°F (220°C) for 10-12 minutes or until crust on bottom is golden brown.

See photograph on page 35.

Cooking time: approximately 12 minutes
1 Large pizza serves 4

Pizza Toppings

Spread Spaghetti Sauce, page 47, over the crust, just enough to cover it. Add your favorite toppings* or use those suggested below. Sprinkle ingredients in layers. The second and third ingredients should be sprinkled over the empty spaces. For a large pizza you will need approximately 3 cups (750 mL) of grated cheese. Use toppings in any combination or amount. Some people like a thin crispy pizza, others enjoy a thick chewy pizza with everything.

Toppings #1 — chopped sliced ham or salami, 3 bacon slices cut into 4 pieces, onion rings, grated mozzarella cheese. Onions should be sautéed in a skillet to half cook them,

Toppings #2 — 3 sausages precooked and sliced, 1 cup (250 mL) sliced mushrooms, 1 large tomato very thinly sliced, grated mozzarella cheese.

Pizza
continued

Toppings #3 — sliced cooked ham, sliced pepperoni sausage, slivered green pepper, grated mozzarella cheese.

Toppings #4 — 2 cooked meatballs; sliced, onions rings partially cooked; 1 large tomato thinly sliced; grated mozzarella cheese.

* Favorite pizza toppings include:

bacon	spiced, cooked	mushrooms	shrimp
ham	ground beef	olives	Cheddar
pepperoni	peppers,	oregano	feta cheese
salami	green or red	basil	mozzarella

Lasagne

8	**lasagne noodles**	8
1½ cups	**Spaghetti Sauce, page 47**	375 mL
¾ cup	**condensed cream of mushroom soup**	175 mL
1 bunch	**fresh spinach or 10 oz. (284 mL) frozen or 14 oz. (398 mL) canned**	1 bunch
12	**mozzarella slices**	12

Cook lasagne noodles according to directions on package. Drain, rinse and drain again. Oil a 12x8" (21x31 cm) pan. Put ⅓ cup (75 mL) of sauce in pan and spread evenly.

First layer: ⅓ of the lasagne noodles, sauce and soup; top with ⅓ of the cheese.

Second layer: all of the spinach, ⅓ of the lasagne noodles, sauce, soup, and cheese.

Third layer: remaining lasagne noodles, sauce, soup; top with remaining cheese.*

Bake on barbecue with lid closed at 325°F (160°C) for 30 minutes.

* Lasagne may be prepared to this stage and refrigerated or frozen until needed. See photograph on back cover.

Cooking time: approximately 30 minutes
Serves 6

Notes

Vegetables

Barbecue Tips on Boiling Vegetables

It does take a while to boil water on the barbecue.

When you need boiling or hot water for cooking, you can do 1 of 3 things:

1) Use hot water from the tap.
2) Heat water in the microwave.
3) Place saucepan on the barbecue 15-30 minutes ahead of time, depending on the amount of water needed and what other foods you are cooking on the barbecue.

Other suggestions you can use:

If you are cooking meat, such as a roast, you may place your pan of water on the barbecue ahead of time and add your vegetables whenever you want to cook them.

Add your vegetables to the boiling water 10 minutes ahead. This is to give time for the water to start boiling again. For example, if it takes potatoes 30 minutes to cook, once they start boiling, allow yourself 40 minutes to cook them.

Follow the direction on your saucepan instructions, so the handles are not being overheated.

Remember not to touch any handles without wearing barbecue or oven mitts.

Barbecue Tips on
Baking Vegetables in Foil

1) Take advantage of your hot barbecue to cook vegetables with your meat — keep your kitchen cool and save energy.

2) Use **heavy-duty** foil always.

3) Fold foil packages securely to seal in cooking juices.

4) Use oven mitts to handle foil packages from barbecue.

Barbecue Tips on
Grilling Vegetables & Fruit

1) Vegetables and Fruit make a quick, flavorful and colorful addition to your barbecue meal.

2) Depending on size and texture (softness), vegetables and fruit may be cooked directly on the grill, threaded on skewers, or cooked in a wire barbecue basket.

3) Prepare vegetables and fruit ahead, wash, peel if necessary, cut to desired size.

4) To baste, use melted butter or a butter and oil combination flavored with herbs or salt and pepper or use Oriental Marinade, page 59, or try some of the flavored Butters, page 64.

5) Suggested vegetables for grilling: tomatoes, sweet (bell) peppers, mushrooms, onion, potatoes, sweet potatoes, squash, eggplant, zucchini, corn-on-the-cob, carrots.

6) Suggested fruits for grilling: pineapple, papaya, bananas (unpeeled), peaches, apples, nectarines, apricots, oranges, melons, pears.

Chicken and Dumplings Stew, page 25
Apple Crisp, page 80
Seasonal Vegetables in Foil, page 55

Seasonal Vegetables in Foil

zucchini, cut in rounds or strips
carrots, thinly sliced
potatoes, sliced or cubed
onions, wedges or slices
broccoli or cauliflower florets
mushrooms, whole or halved
salt and pepper to taste
herbs to taste, 1 or more of parsley,
    dill, oregano, basil, thyme,
    savory, etc.
butter or margarine

Prepare vegetables. Place mixed vegetables on 1 large foil sheet or make serving-size packages. Sprinkle salt, pepper and your favorite herbs over vegetables. Dot with butter. Seal packages securely; barbecue for 20-30 minutes, depending on size.

See photograph on page 53.

Cooking time: 20-30 minutes
Serves — depends on quantities used

Herbed Potatoes in Foil

6	medium potatoes, peeled, cut in bite-sized pieces or sliced	6
2	onions, sliced in rings	2
	salt and pepper to taste	
	herbs to taste, 1 or more of oregano, parsley, dill basil, savory, thyme, chives	
4 tbsp.	soft butter or margarine	60 mL

Place potatoes and onions on 1 or 2 sheets of foil. 2 packages will cook faster. Sprinkle with salt and pepper and your choice of herbs. Dot with butter. Double fold foil and seal ends securely. Place on grill and barbecue for 30-40 minutes. Turn package several times while cooking.

See photograph on front cover.

Cooking time: approximately 30 minutes
Serves 6

Baked Potatoes

Wash potatoes well and remove any blemishes. Puncture potatoes twice with a fork. Wrap each potato individually with foil. Set the barbecue at 350°F (180°C). Bake potatoes with the lid closed. Time as follows:

    large potatoes — 50-60 minutes
    medium potatoes — 40-45 minutes
    small potatoes — 30-35 minutes

Suggested toppings for Baked Potatoes

— butter or margarine
— sour cream or yogurt
— chopped chives, chopped green onions, chopped red onion
— Parmesan cheese, grated Cheddar cheese, crumbled blue cheese, grated Gruyère Cheese, crumbled Feta cheese
— cooked crumbled bacon
— chopped herbs, parsley, dillweed, oregano, basil, marjoram
— steamed or barbecued broccoli or cauliflower florets
— chopped fresh tomato or salsa

Use these toppings alone or in any combination. Stuffed baked potatoes can be a nutritious meal in themselves or a great accompaniment to any main course.

Cooking time: 30-60 minutes
Serves 4

Scalloped Potatoes

4	medium-size potatoes	4
¼ cup	chopped onions	60 mL
	salt	
	pepper	
3 tsp.	all-purpose flour	15 mL
2 cups	milk	500 mL
	parsley	
	paprika	

Butter a 1-quart (1 L) casserole. Slice potatoes ⅛" (3 mm) thick. Layer potatoes and onions; sprinkle each layer with salt, pepper and flour. Do this until casserole is ⅔ full. Add enough milk to just cover the potatoes. Sprinkle with parsley and paprika.

Bake on barbecue with lid down at 350°F (180°C) for 20 minutes, or until potatoes start to boil, then lower heat to 250°F (120°C) for 20-30 minutes, or until potatoes are cooked.

See photograph on page 17.

Cooking time: approximately 40 minutes.
Serves 5

Corn-on-the-Cob in Foil

4-6	ears of corn	4-6
4 tbsp.	soft butter	60 mL
	salt and pepper (optional)	
	chili powder or paprika (optional)	

Remove silk and outer husk from corn. Peel back inner husk but leave attached to the bottom of the cob. Wash corn and remaining husks. Rub soft butter on corn and sprinkle with spices, if desired. Pull husk back up over corn and wrap in foil. Wrap corn individually or 2-3 per package. Barbecue 20-30 minutes, depending on size of package.

Cooking time: 20-30 minutes
Serves 4-6

Baked Beans

2 cups	white beans	500 mL
4 cups	water	1 L
1	small onion, sliced	1
4	thin slices of salt pork	4
¼ cup	molasses	60 mL
2 tbsp.	brown sugar	30 mL
¼ tsp.	pepper	1 mL
1 tsp.	prepared mustard	5 mL

Rinse beans in a strainer/colander under cold water. Transfer to a 1½-quart (1.5 L) saucepan. Add water and let soak overnight.

Drain off soaking water and add fresh water to cover. Place covered saucepan on the barbecue set at 350°F (180°C) with the lid closed. Simmer beans for approximately 45 minutes or until they are getting soft.

Drain beans and keep water. In a crock pot, place ⅓ of the beans. Top with ½ of the onions and ½ of the pork. Add another ⅓ of the beans. Top with remaining onions and pork. Cover with remaining beans.

Mix the next 4 ingredients in the water used for boiling the beans. Pour over beans. If water does not cover beans, add boiling water to cover.

Place covered crock pot on the barbecue. Bake slowly, with lid closed, at 300°F (150°C) for 3 hours. If beans start boiling, lower temperature to 250°F (120°C).

See photograph on front cover.

Cooking time: Approximately 3 hours
Serves 4

Marinades & Sauces

Oriental Marinade

¼ cup	white wine or sherry	60 mL
¼ cup	lemon juice	60 mL
¼ cup	soy sauce	60 mL
¼ cup	vegetable oil	60 mL
2 tbsp.	minced onion	30 mL
2 tsp.	minced fresh ginger	10 mL

Combine all ingredients in a shallow bowl or pan*, or use double plastic bags (check for holes) in a shallow pan. The plastic bags allow you to turn ingredients easily in the marinade.

Use marinade for chicken, beef, pork, fish, vegetables or fruit. Marinate foods to be barbecued for at least 30 minutes to overnight. When ready to barbecue, drain off marinade. Barbecue meat or vegetables and serve hot marinade as a sauce, if you wish.

*For marinades use glass, stainless steel, enamel or plastic containers that won't react with the acids in the marinade.

Yields 1 cup (250 mL)

Teriyaki Marinade

¼ cup	vegetable oil	60 mL
¼ cup	soy sauce	60 mL
¼ cup	sherry or white wine	60 mL
1-2	garlic cloves, minced	1-2
2 tbsp.	minced onion	30 mL
1 tbsp.	grated orange peel	15 mL
1 tsp.	minced fresh ginger	5 mL
	freshly grated pepper, to taste	

Combine all ingredients in a shallow bowl or pan or use double plastic bags (check for holes) in a shallow pan. The plastic bags allow you to turn ingredients easily in the marinade.

Use marinade for beef, pork or chicken. This is wonderful with flank steak. Marinate meat overnight. Drain off marinade and barbecue meat on the grill to your taste.

Yields 1 cup (250 mL)

Citrus Marinade

⅓ cup	vegetable oil	60 mL
½ cup	fresh lime, lemon or orange juice	125 mL
⅓ cup	beer or white wine	75 mL
1 tbsp.	white wine vinegar	15 mL
1 tbsp.	honey	15 mL
¼ cup	finely chopped green onion	60 mL
¼ cup	finely chopped parsley or cilantro	60 mL
1 tbsp.	grated lime, lemon or orange peel	15 mL
1 tbsp.	minced fresh ginger (optional)	15 mL

Combine all ingredients (to vary flavor, try without ginger and with) in a shallow bowl or pan or use double plastic bags (check for holes) in a shallow pan. The plastic bags allow you to turn ingredients easily in the marinade.

Use marinade for fish, shrimp or chicken. Marinate for 30-60 minutes; drain off marinade and barbecue on the grill to your taste.

Yields 1½ cups (375 mL)

Tipsy Barbecue Sauce

¾ cup	ketchup	175 mL
1½ tbsp.	rum or rye	22 mL
½ tsp.	seasoned pepper	2 mL
2 tsp.	Worcestershire sauce	10 mL
1-3 dashes	Tabasco	1-3 dashes

Mix all ingredients together. Seasonings can be adjusted according to taste.

Brown meat on barbecue and then brush on barbecue sauce and continue cooking. This sauce is great for steaks, ribs and pork chops.

Yields ¾ cup (175 mL)

Buttery Herb Baste for Chicken

1 cup	butter or margarine	250 mL
½ cup	lemon juice	125 mL
1 tsp.	dried parsley	5 mL
¼ tsp.	dried sage	1 mL
½ tsp.	dried rosemary	2 mL
½ tsp.	dried thyme	2 mL
¼ tsp.	dried marjoram	1 mL
½ tsp.	dried basil	2 mL
	salt and pepper to taste	

Melt butter in a small saucepan. Add lemon juice, herbs, salt and pepper. Simmer for a few minutes. Dip chicken pieces in warm basting mixture. Place chicken on grill and barbecue to your taste. Baste frequently or, to keep flare-ups to a minimum, remove chicken from grill and redip in sauce 2-3 times.

Yields 1½ cups (375 mL)

Instant Mushroom Sauce

10 oz.	condensed cream of mushroom soup	284 mL
1	garlic clove, minced	5 mL
½ tsp.	tarragon	2 mL
4	mushrooms, chopped	4
1 tbsp.	chives	15 mL

In the top of a double boiler, mix all ingredients together. Simmer for 5-7 minutes. Cover and stir periodically until serving time.

Yields 1⅓ cups (325 mL)

Salmon Sauce

2 tbsp.	butter or margarine	30 mL
3 tbsp.	all-purpose flour	45 mL
⅓ cup	salmon juice*	75 mL
⅔ cup	milk	150 mL
¼ tsp.	prepared mustard	1 mL
⅛ tsp.	pepper	0.5 mL
⅛ tsp.	salt	0.5 mL
⅓ cup	grated cheese	75 mL

In the top of a double boiler, melt margarine. Add flour and mix until smooth. Add salmon juice and milk, slowly stirring until well mixed. Add mustard, pepper, salt and cheese. Stir slowly until cheese is melted and sauce thickens. Cover. Stir periodically until ready to serve.

* Save the juice from canned salmon. If you are using fresh salmon, substitute white wine or fish or chicken stock for salmon juice.

Yields 1⅓ cups (325 mL)

Cheese Sauce

2 tbsp.	margarine	30 mL
2 tbsp.	all-purpose flour	30 mL
1 cup	milk	250 mL
¼ tsp.	prepared mustard	1 mL
pinch	pepper	pinch
pinch	cayenne	pinch
½-1 cup	grated cheese*	125-250 mL

In the top of a double boiler, melt margarine; add flour and stir until well mixed. Add milk, while slowly stirring. Add mustard, pepper and cayenne. Stir until hot and well mixed. Add cheese, stir until cheese is melted and sauce thickens. Cover. Stir periodically until serving time.

* Cheese sauce can be made to your taste by using mild to old cheese. You can also combine 2 or more cheese flavors for variety.

Yields 1½ cups (375 mL)

White Sauce

2 tbsp.	margarine	30 mL
2 tbsp.	all-purpose flour	30 mL
1 cup	milk	250 mL
¼ tsp.	prepared mustard	1 mL
¼ tsp.	salt	1 mL
pinch	pepper	pinch
pinch	cayenne	pinch

In a double boiler, melt margarine, stir in flour, until smooth. Add milk very slowly while stirring. Add remaining ingredients and stir until it thickens. Cover and stir periodically until serving time.

Note: Sauces made in the top of a double boiler will keep very nicely for a few hours. If sauce gets too thick, add milk until it reaches the proper consistency.

Yields 1 cup (250 mL)

Flavored Butters

Add flavored butters to barbecued vegetables, meat and fish; to vegetable and fish packages before barbecuing or top grilled steaks, chops, fish, vegetables and fruit. Store covered, refrigerated, up to 1 week or freeze.

Herbed Butter

½ lb.	butter, room temperature	250 g
6 tbsp.	finely chopped herbs*	90 mL
2 tbsp.	lemon juice	30 mL
2	garlic cloves, minced	2
	freshly ground pepper	

Blend all ingredients in a food processor or electric mixer.

* Try various fresh herb combinations thyme, parsley, dillweed and chives for steaks, chops, chicken or fish; sage, oregano, parsley, basil, marjoram, thyme for chicken, fish or chops.

Yields 1 cup (250 mL)

Lemon Butter

½ lb.	butter, room temperature	250 g
4 tbsp.	fresh lemon juice	60 mL
1 tbsp.	grated lemon rind	15 mL
2 tbsp.	finely chopped parsley	30 mL

Beat together all ingredients. Serve on grilled fish or vegetables.

Variation: for Garlic Lemon Butter, add 2 garlic cloves, minced.

Yields 1 cup (250 mL)

Cheese Butter

½ lb.	butter, room temperature	250 g
3 tbsp.	finely chopped parsley	45 mL
2	garlic cloves, minced	2
	freshly ground black pepper	
⅔ cup	Parmesan Cheese	150 mL

Process all ingredients in a food processor. Serve over seafood, vegetables.

Variation: Blue Cheese Butter, substitute 8 oz. (250 g) blue cheese for Parmesan. Serve over steaks, potatoes, vegetables.

Yields 2 cups (500 mL)

Breads, Muffins & Stuffings

Tea Biscuits

½ cup	shortening	125 mL
2 cups	all-purpose flour	500 mL
3 tsp.	baking powder	15 mL
¾ cup	milk	175 mL

Cut shortening into flour and baking powder with a pastry blender or 2 knifes. Add milk and mix with a fork.

Put dough on lightly floured surface and knead 10-12 times (see page 67 for instructions, How to Knead).

Roll out dough with a rolling pin to about ½" (1 cm) thick. Cut into circles or squares.

Place on ungreased cookie sheet. Preheat barbecue to 375°F (190°C). Elevate cookie sheet on stainless steel rack, see page 6, to prevent burning. Close barbecue cover and bake for 10-12 minutes.

Variations: For Herb Biscuits, add 1-2 tbsp. (15-30 mL) crumbled parsley, oregano or your favorite herbs to the biscuit dough.

See photograph on back cover.

Cooking time: approximately 12 minutes
Makes 10-12 biscuits

Whole-Wheat Biscuits

Prepare above recipe, substituting whole-wheat flour for all-purpose flour.

White Bread

4 tsp.	fast-rising yeast	20 mL
2 cups	warm water	500 mL
1	egg	1
1 tbsp.	soft butter or margarine	15 mL
1 tbsp.	sugar	15 mL
½ tsp.	salt	2 mL
5-6 cups	white, all-purpose flour	1.25-1.5 L

In a large mixing bowl, beat, on high speed, the first 6 ingredients for 1 minute.

Start adding the flour; add 1 cup (250 mL) and beat for about 15 seconds; add 1 more cup (250 mL) and beat until well mixed. Then continue to beat, adding a small amount of flour at a time, approximately ¼ cup (60 mL). Do this until beater starts having difficulty. Continue beating with a wooden spoon, adding flour until dough is very thick and not too sticky. On a counter or table, spread 1 cup (250 mL) flour. Place dough on flour and knead for approximately 5-7 minutes (see page 67 for instructions, How to Knead).

Put dough in a well-greased bowl (remember the bowl has to be big enough for the dough to double in bulk). It will take 20-30 minutes for the dough to rise. Keep it in a warm place and cover with a towel.

While dough is rising, thoroughly grease 2 bread pans.* 10x5x3" (24x13x7 cm).

After dough has risen to twice its volume, roll dough on lightly-floured surface (you can use the same table you used to knead the bread). Cut dough in half; shape each into a loaf, being careful not to handle the dough too much. Put into prepared pans, cover and let stand in warm place to rise again to twice its volume, approximately 20-30 minutes.

Preheat barbecue to 375°F (190°C). Elevate pans on a stainless steel rack, see page 6, to prevent burning. Close barbecue cover and bake for 25-30 minutes. Bread is done when loaves sound hollow when you tap them on top and they are light in weight.

* For campers, use large juice, peanut butter or jam tins to make disposable bread pans.

See photograph on front cover.

Cooking time: approximately 30 minutes
Makes 2 loaves

Whole-Wheat Bread

Make bread the same as previous recipe, White Bread, substituting whole-wheat flour for all-purpose flour. You can also make another variation by using part all-purpose flour and part whole-wheat flour.

See photograph on front cover.

Rolls

Use 1 recipe of White Bread dough and shape dough into small balls. Place balls into greased muffin tins. Let rise until double in bulk, approximately 20-30 minutes. Bake at 350°F (180°) for 20 minutes.

How to Knead

Fold ½ of the dough towards you, then press away from you with the heel of your hands. Give dough a slight turn and press it again. Repeat folding and pressing for about 7 minutes, adding flour if it gets sticky. Kneading is complete when the dough is springy and velvety.

Basic Muffins

3 cups	sour milk	750 mL
3 cups	100% All-Bran	750 mL
3	eggs	3
1 cup	oil	250 mL
¾ cup	brown sugar	175 mL
1 tsp.	vanilla	5 mL
1 tbsp.	baking powder	15 mL
½ tsp.	salt	2 mL
2 tsp.	baking soda	10 mL
3 cups	whole-wheat flour	750 mL

Mix sour milk and bran in a large mixing bowl. Sour milk may be made by adding 1 tsp. (5 mL) vinegar to milk.

In another bowl, beat eggs, oil, sugar and vanilla. Add baking powder, salt, baking soda and ⅓ of the flour; beat well, for about 1 minute. Gradually add remaining flour; beat after every addition. Add flour mixture to bran and milk; mix with a spoon.

To bake, spoon batter into well-greased muffin tins. Fill tins ⅔ full. Preheat barbecue to 350°F (180°C). Elevate muffin tins on a small stainless steel rack, see page 6, to prevent burning. Close barbecue cover. Bake for 20-30 minutes. Muffins are done when a toothpick inserted into the center comes out clean.

Cooking time: approximately 30 minutes.
Makes 30 muffins.

Almond Lemon

To ⅓ of the basic muffin recipe add:

2 tbsp.	grated lemon rind	30 mL
½ cup	slivered almonds	125 mL

Chocolate Chip Coconut

To ⅓ of the basic muffin recipe add:

¾ cup	chocolate chips	175 mL
½ cup	coconut	125 mL

Raisins & Walnut

To ⅓ of the basic muffin recipe add:

¾ cup	raisins	175 mL
½ cup	chopped walnuts	125 mL

Bake as Basic Muffins above. See photograph on page 71.

Pancakes

1	egg	1
1 tbsp.	vegetable oil	15 mL
½ tsp.	salt	2 mL
1 cup	milk	250 mL
1½ cups	all-purpose flour	375 mL
1 tbsp.	baking powder	15 mL
	butter or margarine	

Beat egg with beater; add oil, salt and milk. Beat just enough to mix. Add flour and baking powder; mix with a fork about 15 seconds. Mixture will be lumpy.

Set barbecue to 350°F (180°C) and melt just enough butter or margarine to coat the bottom of the skillet. Spoon batter into skillet; the amount of batter you spoon in depends on how big or thick you want your pancake to be. Cook until you see bubbles on top of the pancake. Turn pancake and cook for 2-3 minutes.

Note: If pancakes brown too quickly, turn down the heat or they won't cook in the middle.

Cooking time: approximately 3 minutes
Makes about 8 medium pancakes

Dumplings

3 tbsp.	shortening	45 mL
2 cups	all-purpose flour	500 mL
3 tsp.	baking powder	15 mL
½ tsp.	salt	2 mL
1 cup	milk	250 mL

Cut shortening into flour, baking powder and salt with 2 knives or a pastry blender. It will look like fine rolled oats. Add milk and mix with a fork. Dough will be very sticky.

Drop dough on top of stew with a fork. Cover pot and simmer for 15 minutes. Keep covered and no peeking please.

Variations: For Herb Dumplings, add 1-2 tbsp. (15-30 mL) crumbled parsley, oregano or your favorite herbs to the dumpling batter.

See photograph on page page 53.

Cooking time: approximately 15 minutes
Makes 8 medium-sized dumplings

Bread Stuffing #1

2 slices	bacon	2 slices
6 slices	4-5-day-old bread, not dry	6 slices
¼ cup	chopped celery	60 mL
2 tbsp.	chopped onions	30 mL
¼ tbsp.	savory	1 mL
⅛ tsp.	thyme	0.5 mL
⅛ tsp.	pepper	0.5 mL
⅛ tsp.	salt	0.5 mL

Precook bacon on barbecue grill, just enough to remove some of the fat. Cut into small pieces (8-10 per slice). Wet bread under hot water tap. Using your hands, squeeze out water and break bread into small pieces in a bowl. Add bacon and all other ingredients. Mix well with your hands.

Use for stuffing chickens or in pork or beef recipes.

Yields approximately 2 cups (500 mL) of stuffing

Bread Stuffing #2

1	chicken neck	1
1	chicken heart	1
1	chicken liver	1
6 slices	4-5-day-old bread, not dry	6
2 tbsp.	chopped onions	30 mL
¼ tsp.	savory	1 mL
⅛ tsp.	poultry seasoning	0.5 mL
¼ tsp.	salt	1 mL
⅛ tsp.	pepper	0.5 mL

In a saucepan, cover chicken neck, liver and heart with water. Simmer for 1 hour. It should not go dry; add some water and keep it simmering.

While meat is simmering, break bread into small pieces in a bowl and add remaining ingredients.

When meat is cooked, chop the liver and heart. Add to bread mixture, along with some of the liquid. Do not use more than ¼ cup (60 mL) of liquid. Mix together with hands or fork.

Use for stuffing chickens, turkeys, ducks or geese.

Yields approximately 2 cups (500 mL) of stuffing

Cheesecake Canadiana, page 77
Almond Lemon Muffins, page 68
Chocolate Chip Muffins, page 68
Coconut, Raisin and Walnut Muffins, page 68
Peanut Butter Cookies, page 78
Drop Cookies, page 78
Old-Fashioned Butter Tarts, page 83
Cranberry Juice

Rice Stuffing #1

1 cup	cooked rice	250 mL
1 cup	mashed potatoes	250 mL
2 tbsp.	chopped green pepper	30 mL
2 tbsp.	chopped onion	30 mL
½ tsp.	salt	2 mL
¼ tsp.	pepper	1 mL
¼ tsp.	savory	1 mL
⅛ tsp.	tarragon	0.5 mL
⅛ tsp.	sweet basil	0.5 mL

In a bowl, mix all ingredients together with a fork.

Use for stuffing chicken or turkey, or stuffed meat loaf and pork recipes that call for stuffing.

Yields 2¼ cups (560 mL)

Rice Stuffing #2

½ cup	wild rice	125 mL
½ cup	white rice	125 mL
3 cups	water	750 mL
2 tbsp.	chopped onions	30 mL
½ tsp.	salt	2 mL
½ tsp.	basil	2 mL
½ tsp.	tarragon	2 mL
¼ tsp.	pepper	1 mL
1 tsp.	sage (optional)	5 mL
1 tsp.	poultry seasoning (optional)	5 mL

Cook all ingredients together in a covered saucepan. Bring to a boil and simmer slowly for 45-60 minutes. Use stuffing for fish, Cornish hens or chickens.

Variations: Try cooking rice in chicken stock instead of water. Add 1 cup (250 mL) sautéed sliced mushrooms to cooked stuffing.

Yields 3 cups (750 mL)

Notes

Desserts

Chocolate Cake

1 cup	sugar	250 mL
½ cup	cocoa	125 mL
1¾ cups	all-purpose flour	425 mL
2 tsp.	baking soda	10 mL
½ cup	vegetable oil	125 mL
2	eggs	2
1 tsp.	vanilla	5 mL
1½ cups	sour milk	375 mL

Grease an 11x9" (26x24 cm) pan and lightly flour the bottom.

In a large mixing bowl combine all dry ingredients. Make a well in the middle and add all the liquids. Beat for 3 minutes, scraping sides of bowl twice.

Pour batter into prepared pan. Preheat barbecue to 350°F (180°C). Bake, elevated on barbecue with lid closed, for 30-40 minutes. Cake is done when a toothpick inserted in center comes out clean.

Cooking time: approximately 40 minutes
Serves 12

White Cake

¾ cup	sugar	175 mL
½ cup	butter or margarine	125 mL
2	eggs	2
1½ cups	flour	375 mL
2 tsp.	baking powder	10 mL
½ cup	sour milk	125 mL
1 tsp.	vanilla	5 mL

Grease an 8" (20 cm) square pan; flour bottom lightly.

In a large mixing bowl, add all ingredients, ending with milk and vanilla. Beat on medium speed for 1 minute. Scrape sides and bottom of bowl. Beat for an additional minute.

Pour batter into prepared pan. Preheat barbecue to 350°F (180°C). Elevate pan on stainless steel rack, see page 6, to prevent burning. Close barbecue lid and bake for 25-35 minutes. Cake is done when a toothpick inserted in the center comes out clean.

Cooking time: approximately 35 minutes
Serves 8

Peanut Butter Icing

4 tbsp.	peanut butter	60 mL
2 tbsp.	butter or margarine	30 mL
⅔ cup	icing sugar	150 mL
2 tbsp.	milk	30 mL

In a small mixing bowl, cream the peanut butter and butter or margarine with a fork or wooden spoon. Add ½ the icing sugar and ½ the milk; mix until smooth.

This amount will frost a 9x9" (23x23 cm) cake. It is very good on either white or chocolate cake.

Cheesecake Canadiana

½ cup	butter or margarine	125 mL
1½ cups	graham wafer crumbs	375 mL
½ tbsp.	unflavored gelatin	7 mL
	(½ envelope)	
8 oz.	cream cheese	250 g
4 tsp.	lemon juice	20 mL
½ cup	sugar	125 mL
1 cup	whipping cream	250 mL
2 cups	fresh strawberries, sliced	500 mL
	strawberry or apple jelly (optional)	

Melt butter or margarine in an 8x11" (20x28 cm) cake pan, on warm barbecue. Mix crumbs in cake pan with melted butter or margarine. Pat crust down with fingers. Bake crust on barbecue on a rack at 350°F (180°C), with lid closed, for 10 minutes; cool.

Meanwhile, dissolve gelatin according to instructions on package. If it hardens, soften over hot water. Beat cream cheese, lemon juice and sugar together until well mixed. Beat whipping cream until it forms a peak. Fold in cheese mixture and add soft gelatin; mix with a spoon or spatula for 15 seconds. Spread over cool crust. Refrigerate overnight or at least 8 hours. Up to this point, it freezes very well.

Cut fresh strawberries into slices. With a toothpick, mark 2 straight lines vertically 1½" (4 cm) from each side of the pan, along the 8" (20 cm) side. In the center, 1½" (4 cm) from each line, etch a maple leaf design of 11 points, plus stem of leaf. Using strawberry slices, cover the 2 rectangular end sections and the maple leaf. Start maple leaf outline, filling in towards the center. You may have to reshape some strawberry slices to avoid gaps and overlapping. Brush strawberry slices with warm, melted strawberry or apple jelly to glaze, if you wish. Thin jelly with water if it is too thick.

The result is a delicious cheesecake with the design of the Canadian flag. You can adapt the decoration of this cheesecake to your own special holiday or family occasion. Use blueberries, red, green or black grapes, kiwi slices, sliced peaches or nectarines or your favorite seasonal fruit.

See photograph on page 71.

Cooking time: approximately 10 minutes
Serves 6

Drop Cookies

1 cup	butter or margarine	250 mL
1 cup	brown sugar	250 mL
2	eggs	2
3 cups	all-purpose flour	750 mL
1 tsp.	baking soda	5 mL
½ tsp.	baking powder	2 mL
¼ tsp.	salt	1 mL
½ cup	chopped walnuts	125 mL
½ cup	chopped coconut	125 mL

Cream margarine and sugar together. Add eggs and beat well. Mix next 4 ingredients together and gradually add to egg mixture. Beat until well mixed. Add walnuts and coconut and fold in with a spoon until mixed.

Drop dough on a greased cookie sheet by spoonfuls about 2" (5 cm) apart. Preheat barbecue to 350°F (180°C). Elevate cookie sheet, see tips page 6. Bake cookies for 12-15 minutes.

See photograph on page 71.

Cooking time: approximately 15 minutes
Makes 36

Peanut Butter Cookies

3 cups	all-purpose flour	750 mL
1 tsp.	baking soda	5 mL
½ tsp.	baking powder	2 mL
¼ tsp.	salt	1 mL
1 cup	butter or margarine	250 mL
¾ cup	peanut butter	175 mL
½ cup	brown sugar	125 mL
½ cup	white sugar	125 mL
2	eggs	2

Mix first 4 ingredients together in a bowl.

In a separate mixing bowl, cream margarine and peanut butter. Add brown and white sugar, and beat until well mixed. Add the eggs and beat well. Gradually add the dry ingredients while beating.

Peanut Butter Cookies
continued

Place tablespoons (15 mL) of batter on an ungreased cookie sheet 2" (5 cm) apart. Press down with a fork dipped in water, to prevent batter from sticking. Bake on barbecue at 350°F (180°C) for 10-12 minutes. Elevate cookie sheet to prevent burning.

See photograph on page 71.

Cooking time: approximately 15 minutes
Makes 48

Chocolate Chip Cookies
Freeze, Slice & Bake

3⅓ cups	all-purpose flour	825 mL
1½ tsp.	baking soda	7 mL
½ tsp.	salt	2 mL
¾ cup	white sugar	175 mL
¾ cup	brown sugar	175 mL
1½ cups	soft butter	375 mL
1½ tsp.	vanilla	7 mL
3	eggs	3
1½ cups	chocolate chips	375 mL
1 cup	unsalted peanuts	250 mL

In a bowl, combine first 3 ingredients and set aside.

In a separate bowl, cream sugars, butter and vanilla. Add eggs and beat well. Gradually add flour mixture and continue beating. Add chocolate chips and mix.

Divide dough into 3 portions. Shape each portion into a roll 1½" (4 cm) in diameter. Roll each one, wrap in wax paper, then freeze. Slice and bake as needed.

Bake on ungreased cookie sheet at 350°F (180°C) for 10 minutes or until golden brown. Remember to elevate the cookie sheet to prevent burning.

See photograph on page 71.

Cooking time: approximately 10 minutes
Makes 48

Apple Crisp

3 cups	sliced apples	750 mL
½ cup	brown sugar	125 mL
¼ tsp.	cinnamon	1 mL
¼ tsp.	nutmeg	1 mL
1 cup	rolled oats	250 mL
¼ cup	all-purpose flour	60 mL
½ tsp.	baking powder	2 mL
3 tbsp.	butter or margarine	45 mL
¼ cup	brown sugar	60 mL

Grease an 8" (20 cm) square pan. Place apples in prepared pan. Add brown sugar over apples. Sprinkle with cinnamon and nutmeg.

In a mixing bowl, combine last 5 ingredients and mix with a pastry blender. Sprinkle evenly over apples.

Bake, elevated, on barbecue at 375°F (190°C) for 20 minutes. Lower heat to 250°F (120°C) and cook 30 minutes more.

Variations: Make your favorite Fruit Crisp: Substitute 3 cups (750 mL) of sliced pears, plums, peaches, blueberries, rhubarb (add ½ cup [125 mL] of sugar, or to taste) or pitted cherries for the apples. Also try ½ or ⅔ rhubarb combined with strawberries.

See photograph on page 53.

Cooking time: approximately 50 minutes
Serves 6

Bibianne says: Not enough space in the oven? Bake some of your dishes on the barbecue!

Pie Crust/Pastry

3 cups	all-purpose flour	750 mL
1 cup	cold shortening	250 mL
½ tsp.	baking powder	5 mL
2 tbsp.	cold butter or margarine	30 mL
½ cup	cold water	125 mL

In a mixing bowl, combine flour, shortening, baking powder and butter or margarine. Mix with a pastry blender until it looks like fine rolled oats.

Note: Mix will keep very well, refrigerated, for 1 month or 6 months frozen.

Make a well in the middle and add ½ of the water. Mix pastry with a fork; you may need more water.

To make pie crust, put a 1-crust portion of pastry on a floured board. With the use of a rolling pin coated with flour, roll dough large enough to cover pie plate. Line pie plate with pastry.

Put filling in crust, then roll enough pastry to cover pie.

Note: When adding water, dough will be slightly sticky. If it is too sticky when you roll it out on a floured surface, add more flour.

Note: To make pastry leaves or fruit to decorate pie crusts, roll out scraps of dough. Cut out desired shapes with a knife or cookie cutter. Brush top crust lightly with milk and apply pastry decorations. Brush decorations with milk and sprinkle with white sugar to glaze. Bake as instructed in the pie recipe.

See photograph on pages 17 and 71.

Makes 3 double-crust pies

Apple Pie

	pastry for a 2-crust, 9" (23 cm) pie	
6-8	medium-sized apples	6-8
¾ cup	brown sugar	175 mL
½ tsp.	cinnamon	2 mL
½ tsp.	nutmeg	2 mL
1 tbsp.	butter or margarine	15 mL
1 tsp.	milk	5 mL

Prepare pastry. Line pie plate with bottom crust. Peel, core and slice apples, place in pie crust. Add sugar, sprinkle with cinnamon and nutmeg. Dab butter or margarine 4-5 places on apples. Cover with top crust. Cut vents in top crust for steam to escape.*

Brush milk over crust. Bake, elevated, on barbecue at 400°F (200°C), with lid closed, for 15 minutes or until it starts to brown. Lower heat to 350°F (180°C) and bake for ½ hour.

* At this stage pie may be frozen and baked when needed.

Cooking time: approximately 45 minutes
Makes 1 pie

Blueberry Pie

	pastry for a 2-crust, 9" (23 cm) pie	
4 cups	fresh blueberries	1 L
¾ cup	sugar	175 mL
1 tbsp.	all-purpose flour	15 mL
1 tsp.	milk	5 mL

Prepare pastry. Line pie plate with bottom pie crust. Add blueberries. Combine sugar and flour and sprinkle over berries. Cover with top crust. Cut vents for steam to escape.*

Brush top crust with milk. Bake, elevated, on barbecue at 400°F (200°C), with lid closed, for 15 minutes or until pie starts to brown. Lower heat to 350°F (180°C) and bake for ½ hour.

* At this stage pie may be frozen and baked when needed.

See photograph on page 17.

Cooking time: approximately 45 minutes
Makes 1 pie

Sugar Pie

pastry for 1-crust, 8-9"
(20-23 cm) pie

2½ cups	brown sugar	625 mL
3 tbsp.	all-purpose flour	45 mL
½ cup	cereal cream (10%)	125 mL
1 tsp.	vanilla	5 mL

Prepare pastry. Line pie plate with pastry. Over prepared pie crust, sprinkle sugar and flour; mix carefully with a fork. Gently pour cream over the sugar; drizzle vanilla over cream.

Bake, elevated, on barbecue at 400°F (200°C), with lid closed, for 5 minutes. Reduce temperature to 350°F (180°C) and bake for 20 minutes. Pie is done when filling looks like thick custard.

Cooking time: approximately 40 minutes
Makes 1 pie

Old-Fashioned Butter Tarts

1 cup	raisins	250 mL
1 cup	butter or margarine	250 mL
1 cup	brown sugar	250 mL
1 tsp.	vanilla	5 mL
2	eggs	2
	tart shells	

Rinse raisins in colander/strainer under hot water tap and let drain.

Cream butter or margarine; add sugar and beat until fluffy. Add vanilla and eggs, beat until fluffy; add raisins.

Fill tart shells ⅔ full. Elevate tarts on rack approximately 2" (5 cm) in height. Bake on barbecue at 375°F (190°C), with lid closed, for 15-18 minutes.

Note: tarts are cooked when crust is golden brown and filling is medium brown on top.

See photograph on page 71.

Cooking time: approximately 18 minutes
Makes 32 small or 20 large tarts

INDEX

85

Share *Barbecue Chez Bibianne* with a friend

Order *Barbecue Chez Bibianne* at $8.95 per book, plus $2.00 (total order) for shipping and handling.

Barbecue Chez Bibianne _____ x $8.95 = _____ $ _____

Add shipping and handling charge_____ $ _____ $2.00

Subtotal_____ $ _____

In Canada add 7% Goods & Services Tax (GST) _____(Subtotal x .07) $ _____

Total enclosed _____ $ _____

U.S. and International orders payable in U.S. Funds

Name _____

Street _____City _____

Province/State _____Postal Code/Zip Code _____

Make cheque payable to: **Chez Bibianne Enterprises Inc.**
P.O. Box 50041
14061 Victoria Trail
Edmonton, Alberta
Canada T5Y 2M9

For fund-raising or volume purchases, contact Chez Bibianne Enterprises Inc. for volume rates.

Please allow 3-4 weeks for delivery. Price is subject to change.

Share *Barbecue Chez Bibianne* with a friend

Order *Barbecue Chez Bibianne* at $8.95 per book, plus $2.00 (total order) for shipping and handling.

Barbecue Chez Bibianne _____ x $8.95 = _____ $ _____

Add shipping and handling charge_____ $ _____ $2.00

Subtotal_____ $ _____

In Canada add 7% Goods & Services Tax (GST) _____(Subtotal x .07) $ _____

Total enclosed _____ $ _____

U.S. and International orders payable in U.S. Funds

Name _____

Street _____City _____

Province/State _____Postal Code/Zip Code _____

Make cheque payable to: **Chez Bibianne Enterprises Inc.**
P.O. Box 50041
14061 Victoria Trail
Edmonton, Alberta
Canada T5Y 2M9

For fund-raising or volume purchases, contact Chez Bibianne Enterprises Inc. for volume rates.

Please allow 3-4 weeks for delivery. Price is subject to change.